Business Acumen: Business Plan

Written by: brendon thutso
2020

Table of contents

Introduction

Objectives:

- ❖ To explain how a business plan is essential in creating a successful business
- ❖ To know how to write a business plan
- ❖ To learn the steps of starting a business
- ❖ To learn more about the structure of businesses
- ❖ To acquire more skills and knowledge about business and business strategies

Business Acumen: Business Plan (Introduction)

We are in an era where business makes the world go round. Everybody wants to start their own business and be successful but then they realize that succeeding in business is as hard as trying to fit a log of wood in a needle hole. Failing in business does not mean one is a failure or loser; it just means that they lack planning and strategizing which are the main skills one will acquire after reading this book.

When starting a business, it is always important to plan your business, to brainstorm and to visualize it beforehand so that you don't waste time, money, opportunities and your own resources. The best way to plan for success in business is through a **business plan**. A business plan is a written description of your business's future, a document that tells what you plan to do and how you plan to do it. If you jot down a paragraph on the back of an envelope describing your business strategy, you've written a plan, or at least the germ of one. Business plans are inherently strategic.

Having the ability to write a business plan makes all the paths to having a successful business lucid.

Most successful businesses in the world are guided by a business plan. It has been proven that a business with a business plan is likely to grow 25% more and faster than a business without a plan. A business plan shows the vision, goals, maximum potential and objectives of a business hence it is the core of a business. People with business plans attract investors because investors feel safe trusting their money to a business that is organized, strategic and also productive.

Below is a graph that compares the growth and opportunities secured by a business with a business plan vs one without.

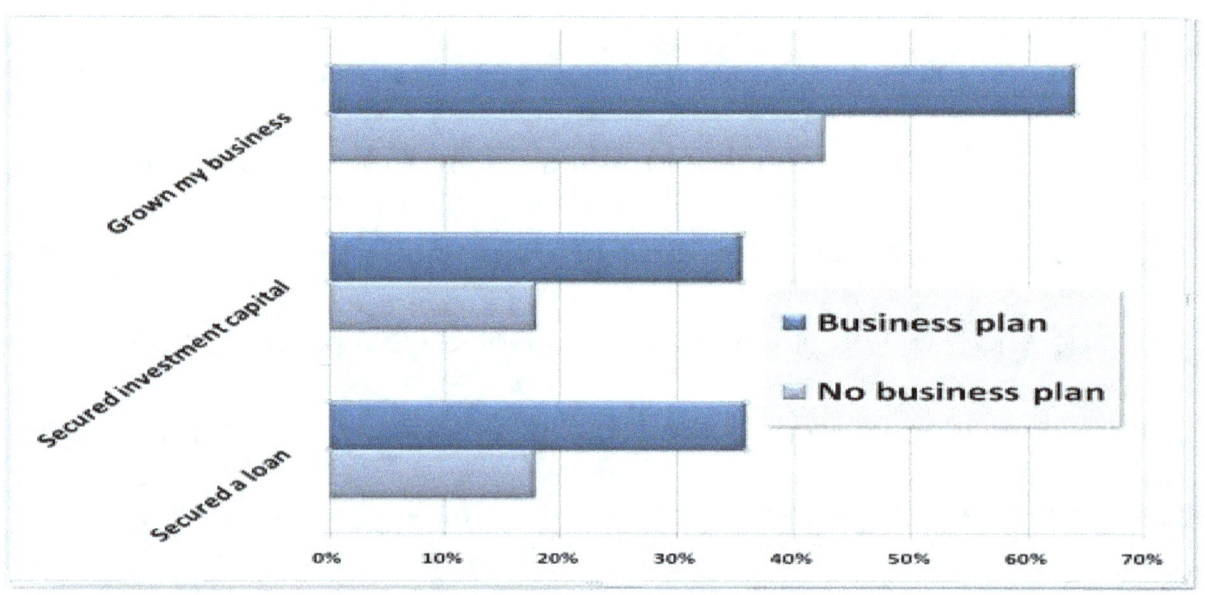

This graph proves how essential it is to have a business plan because it leads to a more successful business.

Uses of a business plan

Objectives:

- ❖ To state the uses of a business plan
- ❖ To explain why the business plan is essential in business
- ❖ To explain the link between a business plan and the success of a business

USES OF A BUSINESS PLAN:

1. **It helps you visualize your business**

   - Visualizing your business because commencing it is very important because it helps you foresee all the challenges and merits you are likely to face in the future. It also helps determine if you are going about the right direction to building a successful business or not.

2. **It can attract investors and help you acquire loans**

   - When you present a business plan to potential investors or lenders it gives them the impression that you are organized and that you have a vision. They can be able to trust you with their money because the business plan simplifies and explains your forecast and objectives and how you are going to execute the business. It will also help you acquire suitable loans because all figures are accounted for.

3. It can minimize losses

- The worst enemy of a business is a loss, and although they can be almost inevitable at times, a business plan can help you execute how the losses can be reduced or avoided. So having a business plan is essential for a profitable company

4. Leads to an organized business

- A haphazard business is likely to face unreasonable losses, lose customers, investors, and also to decline. To avoid having an unorganized business, it is delicate to have a business plan because it encompasses all the details on how you are going to organize your business.

5. Helps manage business income and expenses

- A successful business has more income than expenses. So for you to avoid having more expenses a business plan is needed because it will help navigate all business strategies in order to gain more income. Once a company has more expenses than the income it can decline because the income will help pay off the expenses with no profit to keep the business running

6. Guides in marketing the business and expanding clients

- A business plan has a section dedicated to marketing which describes how the business will be exposed to a broad range of markets. So a business plan will help plan out how the potential clients will be turned to buying clients.

7. It leads to a successful business

- A business plan is a vision of the business. It can help visualize the maximum potential of a business. The success of all businesses is determined by the plan. So a well-executed business plan can help manifest the full potential of a business. The reason why most businesses fail is that they don't have a business plan. With a business plan, any business can be a powerhouse in the blink of an eye.

Components of a business plan

Objective:

- ❖ To know all peripherals of a business plan

- ❖ To define and explain the sections of a business plan

- ❖ To know how to structure and lay out a business plan

- ❖ To learn the format of accounting books

Topics:

2.1 Business plan cover

2.2 An executive summary

2.3 Opportunity explanation

2.4 Execution

2.5 Milestones and metrics

2.6 Company structure

2.7 Financial plan

2.8 Statements

COMPONENTS OF A BUSINESS PLAN

A business plan is simply the written structure and the backbone of any business. It encompasses all strategies, accounts, summaries, equipment, and peripherals of the business.

The business plan consists of:

- Business plan cover

- An executive summary

- Opportunity explanation

- Execution

- Milestones and metrics

- Company structure

- Financial plan

- Statements

Business plan cover (2.1)

This is the first page of a business plan and it gives the first impression and general details of your business.

The cover should include:

- **The logo** of your business should be strategically placed such that it is the highlight of the page. There are many ways to acquire a logo. These may include specifically designing the logo, using applications that can design a logo for you, paying a professional to design a logo for you, and even buying an already made logo. Usually, businesses get stuck with copyright infringements because they use other companies' logos which is bad for business, so make sure that your logo is unique and does not belong to anyone but your company.

- **The name of the business**. This also should be strategically placed such that it is a highlight of the page. Preferably, it should have a large font and bold, because the name of the business is the face of business. Just like with the logo, a business can be struck with copyright infringement if they use another business's name, so make sure that your business has its own unique name, besides, having a basic business name or a name that most businesses have can be bad for marketing because once a client searches for your

business in the internet, and your business is buried within other businesses

they are likely to go with the other businesses.

- **The preparer of the business plan**. This includes the name(s) of the

person(s) who created the business plan and the contact details {phone

number and email address)

- **The date when the plan was created**. This doesn't have to be a specific

date. You can just write the year the plan was created.

- **The header and footer**. The header usually includes the business name and

page number. The footer includes a copyright notice, which explains that the

plan can't be read or disseminated without consent from the plan creator.

Executive summary (2.2)

The executive summary is the definition or a brief explanation of the whole plan. The executive summary includes:

- **The problem summary**. This is a brief description of the problem worth solving or the problem that your company is going to solve. For example: if there is a shortage of commodities that you would be able to offer, then you define it in a few words.

- **The solution summary**. This is the brief description of how you would solve the defined problems in a few sentences. For example, if there is a shortage of commodities, you now explain how you are going to end the shortage and provide the commodities.

- **The market**. This includes the target market. The clientele that you will offer the services or goods to.

- **Competition.** This is where you state your key competition. You briefly state without explaining whom your customers might consider. This does not necessarily have to be company names, you'd rather state it as categories. For example, educational institutions, local restaurants, airports etc, in that way no one is blacklisted.

- **The merits of your business**. This is where you state why your business stands out from other businesses. You justify why people should choose your business and not your competitors. This section should be just straightforward unexplained points. In simpler terms, state the advantages of your company.

- **Expectations.** This is where you state the forecast of the business. In general, you are stating what you expect your business to be like in the future. Some of the primary points may include the expansion of the business to a wide range of clientele and paying off most if not all liabilities

- **Financing.** This is where you state the means of obtaining the capital. That can include loans, savings, fundraising, and many other means you can think of to obtain money to commence your business. And then you state the range of money that you'll need to raise to commence the business.

Opportunity explanation (2.3)

This section is for explaining everything stated in the executive summary and also to further elaborate on the strategies of the business and the outcome.

The opportunity explanation includes:

- **The problem.** This is where you define the problem that your business is there to solve. So if there is a lack in a commodity you explain that lack and its effects on the community or on the designated market that your business targets. Basically you expand on the points stated in the "problem summary" and further elaborate.

- **The solution.** This is where you elaborate how you will solve the problem by providing your goods and services. You explain how your service will improve the situation in the targeted market and quench the problem stated.

- **Target market.** In the section you define and explain your market size and segment. You have to explain who you have targeted as a potential client and where they are and how your business is situated such that you have access to them and they can also easily access you.

- **Competition.** The main challenge of any business is their competition. So you have to state and explain who is in the same business as you, who offers services and products similar or congruent to yours and who supplies clients the commodities you supply and explain how you are unique and better than them.

- **The business advantages.** This is where you explain and elaborate on why your business is better than your competition. Further state how your services are better than your competition. Explain what you have to offer that they don't offer. Basically this is supporting your services. Expanding on how unique they are and how they solve problems in the area. This section is important because it builds the credibility of your plan and guides you every time you execute your plans.

Execution (2.4)

The general definition of execution is to carry out a plan or to implement a plan. So in the section of our business plan we express how we implement the plan.

The peripherals of this section include:

- **The marketing plan**. Marketing is the brain of the business. Good marketing skills lead to a flourishing business but little to no marketing will lead to the decline of the business. In the marketing plan you have to write what you are going to implement so that the business reaches a broad range of your target market. You have to strategize and raise awareness of your business and also in the process form the credibility of your business. Some of the marketing strategies to include in the marketing plan include:

- Circulating your business cards

- Creating posters with business information

- Creating media advertisements

- Exploiting social networking sites by sharing your business and services

- Handing out flyers, etc

The marketing plan can be divided into direct and indirect marketing. Direct marketing refers to proposing your services to clients through direct communication, for example, speaking on the phone or in person. Whereas with indirect marketing you don't talk to the customer but your actions can showcase your business and then attract the customer. For example adverts in video skits. Conclusively, strong and organized marketing skills lead to the success of your business, so spend most of your time polishing up your marketing plan.

- **Sales plan**. In this section of the plan you have to write how you are going to turn random people or potential clients into buying customers. This section works hand-in-hand with marketing because for a person to turn into a buying customer your marketing has to assure them that you are highly credible and reliable. Usually with the sales plan you should be able to come up with how you will mainly attract people to trust your services. It is generally encompassing of the marketing plan and your business solution.

- **Operations**. This is a broad segment because it encompasses the whole structure of the business. From how the business is situated to what the peripherals of the business are. It includes:

  - The location and facilities of the business. This encompases where the business is located from your target market, how the building of the business is and also how close the business is to resources that keep the business running.

- Technology. Technology encompases the hardware and softwares of the business. i.e. the business ticketing systems, online presence and accessibility, banking system, barcode reading and print. So all the technological components are stated in this section

- Equipment and tools. These should be parts that keep the business running. They usually include assets like furniture, vehicles, and so forth. For example, if you are running an industry, you'd have to state the machinery of the business.

Milestones and metrics (2.5)

Milestones of the business refers to what you hope your business achieves in the future. It encompasses the goals that you hope your business will reach in a given time in the future, this can be days, months, years or even decades.

Then, metrics refers to how you will know that your business is successful or moving in the right direction. So tallying it with the milestones. The metrics of the business refer to the fulfillment of the milestones or the forecast you have for the business.

It is very delicate to have milestones for the business because it will give you a motive to work towards and once you reach the metrics you will be able to know that your business is moving in the right direction.

Company structure (2.6)

Business structures include: sole proprietorship, partnership, corporation and limited liability company. So with the structure of the business you have to explain the ownership and management of the business, how the funds will be distributed towards the inputs and processes of the business, who the team is going to include and also the duties of the team.

This section includes:

- **The overview**. Explain the structure of your company, if it's sole owned or a partnership and how the company will be run.

- **Team**. This will include the management team, the legal team and the advising team. All these aspects are necessary to run a successful business.

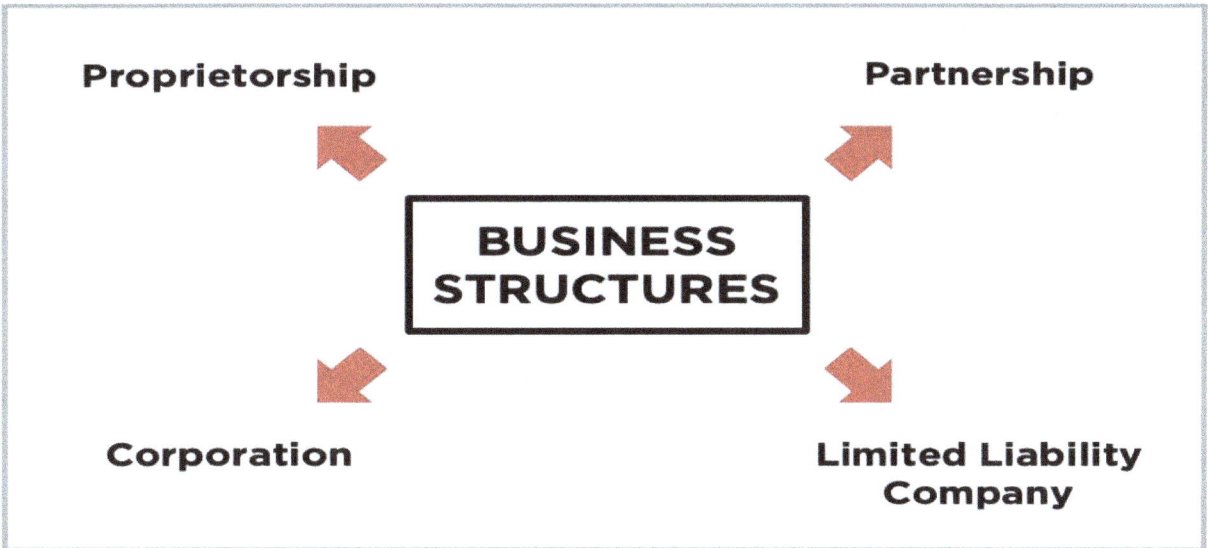

Financial plan (2.7)

This section of the business plan encompasses all the monetary aspects of the business. This includes the financial forecasts and financial state of the business.

The peripherals of the financial plan include:

- **Key assumption.** In this section all the capital of the business has to be accounted for. You have to express clearly where the capital will come from and how it is going to be used to execute the input and processes of the business. Then a brief statement on the expenses of the company should be written too and how long it will take for the liabilities to be paid back. Then also a statement about how profits will be utilized should be recorded in this section.

- **Revenue by month.** With the revenue or income of the business you can not be sure how much you'll receive but you can decipher and estimate how much the business can make in a month. So you can account for the twelve months of the year how the business is going to perform financially also stating where the revenue comes from. A chart is needed to present the information you write down. The chart should present how much the business will make each month each month.

- **Expenses by month**. It's also almost impossible to know all the expenses of a business accurately because expenses accumulate by day. So you'll have to write the possible expenses of the business and account for them. The graph has to show the expenses amount of a month(s). Every business has expenses so it's a great idea to account for them so that you'll be able to execute through the revenue, capital and the expenses during the business process.

- **Net profit or loss by year**. Profit or losses are a result of revenue less the expenses of the business. A chart that represents the profits and losses for the whole year is essential to visualize the finances of the business.

- **Financing**. This section further elaborates on the use and sources of funds. It should explain how the funds will cover the expenses, the liabilities and all other processes of the business. So if the finances are distributed towards certain activities it should be recorded in this section.

Statements (2.8)

A business plan with statements is 500% more likely to attract investors than a business plan that doesn't have one. This section is the accounting and arithmetic section of the business.

The statements of the business plan encompass:

- the projected profit and loss,

- the projected balance sheet

- and the projected cash flow statements.

Each of these statements are important to showcase and summarize every information in the business plan.

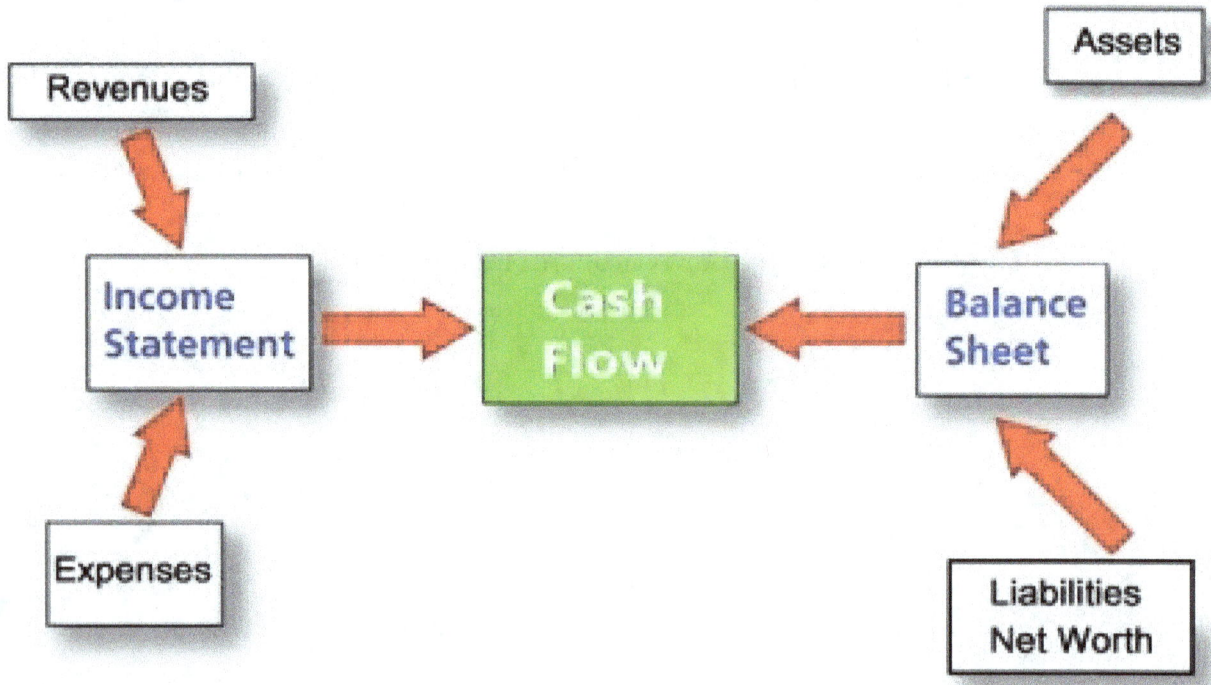

Projected profit and loss

This statement shows the company revenue and expenses in a given period of time.

It shows how the revenue can be turned into the net income over time. Below is the

structure of the profit and loss statement showing all aspects of obtaining the net

income of a company. Study it and know it, it is essential for your business.

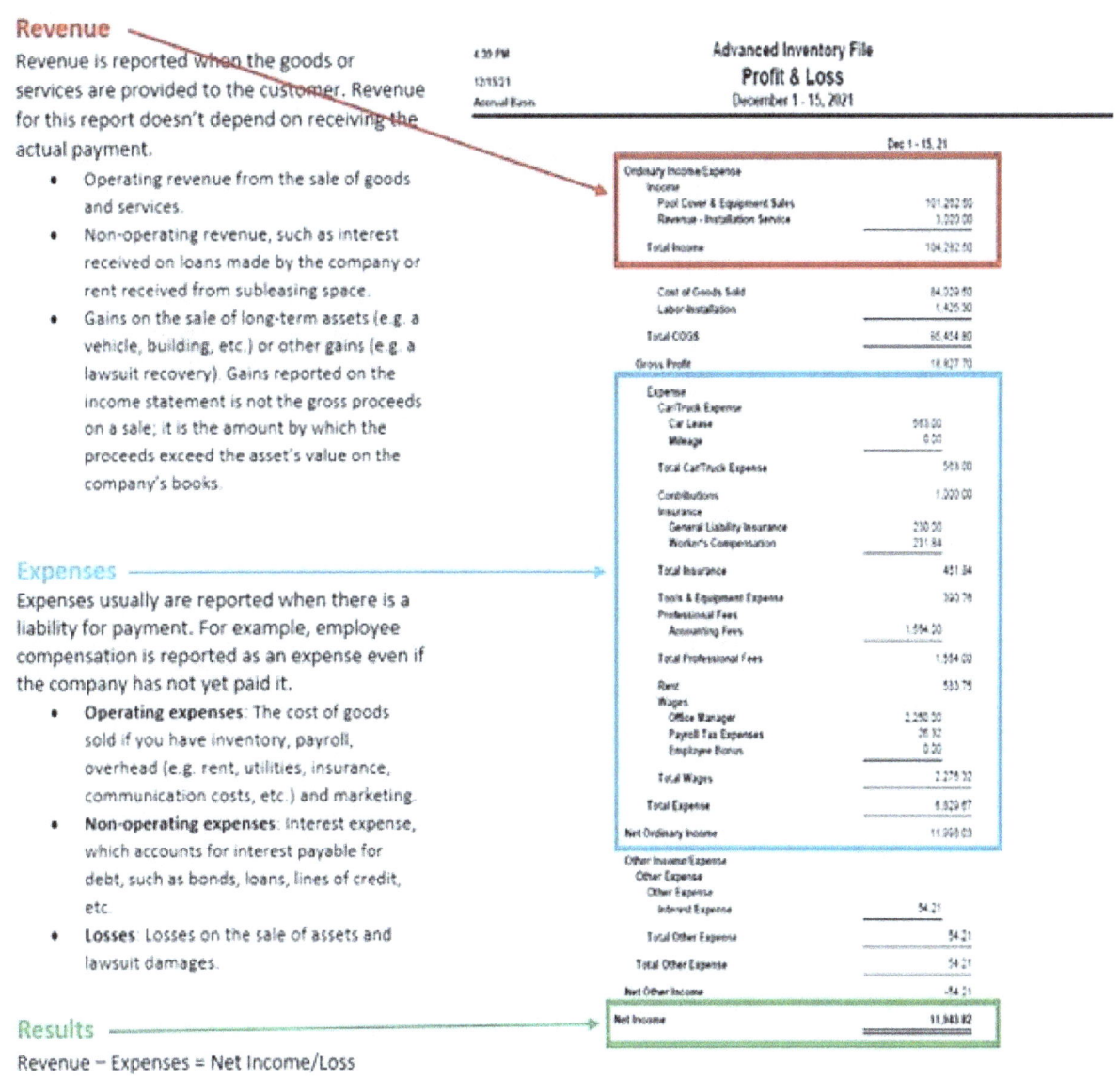

Revenue

Revenue is reported when the goods or services are provided to the customer. Revenue for this report doesn't depend on receiving the actual payment.

- Operating revenue from the sale of goods and services.
- Non-operating revenue, such as interest received on loans made by the company or rent received from subleasing space.
- Gains on the sale of long-term assets (e.g. a vehicle, building, etc.) or other gains (e.g. a lawsuit recovery). Gains reported on the income statement is not the gross proceeds on a sale; it is the amount by which the proceeds exceed the asset's value on the company's books.

Expenses

Expenses usually are reported when there is a liability for payment. For example, employee compensation is reported as an expense even if the company has not yet paid it.

- **Operating expenses**: The cost of goods sold if you have inventory, payroll, overhead (e.g. rent, utilities, insurance, communication costs, etc.) and marketing.
- **Non-operating expenses**: Interest expense, which accounts for interest payable for debt, such as bonds, loans, lines of credit, etc.
- **Losses**: Losses on the sale of assets and lawsuit damages.

Results

Revenue – Expenses = Net Income/Loss

Projected balance sheet

This is one of the final books in a business plan. It is the summary of the financial balances of the business. It includes the capital, assets and all liabilities of the company and totals them all up. This book describes all the monetary aspects of your business and it determines whether your business is running positively or negatively. So this projection should be able to summarize all the assets the business already has, the capital the business has or is to have, and all the liabilities the business will face or already faces. Below is the model of a balance sheet. Study it and master it. It is vital for the business.

Balance Sheet for Nautilus Hosting

Assets

What you own or control, such as cash on hand, money that you expect to collect from customers, inventory, company vehicles, and money in the bank.

Assets	
Cash and bank	$123,967.11
Other current assets	$37,510.80
Long term assets	$0.00
Long term assets	**$161,477.91**

The value of everything you own or control.

Liabilities

What you owe, such as debts, loans, or credit cards, wages and salaries, rent and utilities, money owed to suppliers, and taxes.

Liabilities	
Current liabilities	$5,083.56
Long term liabilities	$13,560.00
Total liabilities	**$18,643.56**

The cost of everything you owe.

Equity

What you own and control minus what you owe. Your piece of the business holdings after paying your debts.

Equity	
Retained earnings	$142,834.35
Total equity	**$142,834.35**

The value of your assets minus your liabilities.

Projected cash flow statement

A cash flow statement is a financial statement that summarizes the amount of cash and cash equivalents entering and leaving the business. The cash flow statement measures how well the business manages its cash position and how well the company generates cash to pay its debt obligations and fund for its operating expenses. So this projection should reflect how the business manages its finance position. A format of the cash flow statement is below.

Format for Cash Flow Statement

Cash flows from operating activities		
(List of individual items)	XX	
Net cash provided (used) by operating activities		XXX
Cash flows from investing activities		
(List of individual inflows and outflows)	XX	
Net cash provided (used) by investing activities		XXX
Cash flows from financing activities		
(List of individual inflows and outflows)	XX	
Net cash provided (used) by financing activities		XXX
Net increase (decrease) in cash		XXX
Cash at beginning of period		XXX

Using a business plan to get funds

Objectives:

- ❖ To learn how to acquire funds for business using a business plan
- ❖ To know who to present the business plan to for funds
- ❖ To learn how to strategically write the plan to attract lenders
- ❖ To know the essence of a business plan in acquiring funds
- ❖ To understand the most vital sections of a business plan

Why you need a business plan to get funds

The most essential aspect of starting a business is having sufficient capital to commence it. Without capital the business has the most slim chances to succeed. It is not easy to raise capital but the good news is that your business plan makes it very possible and less hard to obtain capital in numerous ways. The business plan appeals in so many ways in the eyes of lenders, investors and funders. Some of the reason include:

It helps lenders know more about your business. The first part that the lenders will look at in your business plan is the executive summary and if it appeals to them they will want to know more and they might want to invest because they know what your business is about

It shares your business goals and objectives. Nobody would ever entrust their money to a person without any goals and objectives. The goals of a business unravel the future and vision of the business and that is what the business plan contains

It proves that you are organized. It is easier to trust an organized person because they have a certain sequence that they follow. Therefore having a business plan is a sign of being organized and it appeals most to the lenders.

It shares the current and needed finances. Lenders are attracted to an upfront person and the business plan can prove that you are upfront because it shows the financial state of the business and also how much you need at the moment. So the lenders don't waste time trying to guess how much you need

It is more informative than the word of mouth. Usually when you talk about your business you can forget a lot of things unlike when they are written down and summed up. Thus when you talk about your business there are some things that you are not able to say but that a business plan can represent lucidly, for example, graphs and tables.

Where to present your business plan

Since a business plan gives you a broad range of opportunities in acquiring funds, let's explore where you can present your business plan to acquire funds.

- **Banks.** Most banks are always looking for new businesses to invest in, but they don't just pick anyone and everyone. They assess your plan and also the goals and objectives of your business. So it is important to have a business plan because it will cover all the aspects that banks require in a business they want to invest in.

- **Private companies**. Some companies look for opportunities where they can gain rather than to lose money. So they have to know who they risk their money to and also the information of what they risk their money in. so it is essential to have the business plan at hand so that they understand your plan and be assured that they won't lose their money.

- **Investment organizations.** Most organizations are willing to invest in a business that is organized, so it is essential to have a business plan. Most investment organizations offer long term loans all depending on the agreements.

- **Credit unions.** Credit unions provide loans at reasonable rates, so it is always a great idea to explore through them if you are looking for business funds. Always have the business plan to present.

- **Payday lenders.** These lenders offer short term loans with high interest rates but they make the process of acquiring the funds faster. The memo of the loan note will require information from your business plan so always have it at hand.

One page business plan (brainstorming)

Objectives:

- ❖ To learn how to brainstorm a business idea before transferring it to the business plan

- ❖ To learn how to draft the key elements of a business plan

- ❖ To know the main structure of the business.

Simple brainstorm business plan

To brainstorm your idea before putting it in the official business plan is essential. The best way to brainstorm a business idea is to use a one page business plan. This consists of the most essential peripherals of the plan and you can fill it in with brief points. The next 2 pages consist of the structure of the one page business plan that you can use to brainstorm any business plan that you have.

Basically the one page business plan consists of :

- General details (name, date, contacts)

- Problem worth solving

- solution

- Sales & marketing

- Milestones & metrics

- Business model

The next two pages have the model of the one page business plan. Use them and brainstorm any business ideas you have and briefly fill in the strategies you will execute.

One Page Business Plan

Company Name:

Web Site:	Name:	Phone:
Twitter:	Title:	Industry:
Facebook:	Email:	Stage:

Problem (what pain is your biz is solving?)

Solution (how is your biz solving that?)

Impact (what is the positive social impact of your biz?)

Business Model (how does your biz make money?)

Secret Sauce (what is the underlying magic?)

Sales & Marketing (how will your biz go to market?)

Competition (what your biz can do they can't?)

Team (who is on your team, why are they good?)

Projections & Milestones (underlying important metrics)

Status & Timeline (where is the biz now?)

Next Steps #1	Next Steps #2	Next Steps #3

One Page Business Plan

Company Name:

Web Site: Name: Phone:

Twitter: Title: Industry:

Facebook: Email: Stage:

Problem (what pain is your biz is solving?)

Solution (how is your biz solving that?)

Impact (what is the positive social impact of your biz?)

Business Model (how does your biz make money?)

Secret Sauce (what is the underlying magic?)

Sales & Marketing (how will your biz go to market?)

Competition (what your biz can do they can't?)

Team (who is on your team, why are they good?)

Projections & Milestones (underlying important metrics)

Status & Timeline (where is the biz now?)

Next Steps #1   Next Steps #2   Next Steps #3

Business plan guideline template

Objective:

❖ To guide the learner in the step of creating a business plan

❖ To know all the peripherals of a business plan

❖ To understand finances and strategies of business

❖ To understand accounting books

❖ To visualize a business guided by the template

Executive Summary

Opportunity

Problem Summary

INSTRUCTIONS: Describe very briefly why your business needs to exist. What

problem do you solve for your customers?

Solution Summary

INSTRUCTIONS: Briefly summarize what your company does. The executive

summary should be very short and you can go into more detail later in the plan.

Market

INSTRUCTIONS: Describe your target customer or market segments. Again, keep

things very brief in the executive summary and add more detail later in the plan.

Competition

INSTRUCTIONS: Summarize your key competition. Who will your customers

also consider?

Why Us?

INSTRUCTIONS: Write a brief overview of you and your team. Why are you the

right people to build this business?

Expectations

Forecast

INSTRUCTIONS: Write a brief overview of your financial targets. How much do you plan to sell in the next year? What are your long-term sales goals?

Financial Highlights by Year

INSTRUCTIONS: Insert a chart of your key financial metrics here.

Financing Needed

INSTRUCTIONS: If you are writing a business plan to raise money for your business, include a brief summary of what you are looking for. If you aren't raising money or getting a loan, you can delete this section.

Opportunity

Problem & Solution

Problem Worth Solving

INSTRUCTIONS: Write a little more detail than you provided in the Executive Summary about the problem you are solving. What do your customers need? Do they need a better product, a cheaper product, or just a store in a better location? Describe why customers will want to buy from you.

Our Solution

INSTRUCTIONS: Provide additional detail, beyond what you wrote in the Executive Summary, about your product or service. What is unique and special about your company that's going to set it apart from the competition?

Target Market

Market Size & Segments

INSTRUCTIONS: Describe your key customers – who they are and what their key attributes are. If your company is targeting multiple customer groups (also called 'segments'), describe each group here. If you can, include details about how many people are in each segment and how large the total market is.

Competition

Current Alternatives

INSTRUCTIONS: Describe your current competition. What products and services are people using instead of yours?

Our Advantages

INSTRUCTIONS: Explain why your product or service is better than the others. Also, be sure to describe any competitive advantages you may have, such as a patent or other unique component to your business.

Execution

Marketing & Sales

Marketing Plan

INSTRUCTIONS: Explain how you plan on getting the word out about your product to your target market(s). Will you use advertising? Perhaps you are developing a content marketing strategy. Whatever your marketing plans may be, describe them here.

Sales Plan

INSTRUCTIONS: If your company relies on sales people to close sales deals, you need a sales plan. Your sales plan should explain how you convert people who express interest in your product or service into paying customers. If you are opening a food truck, this section is less important and you can consider removing it. However, if you are starting a sales-heavy business like enterprise software or a car dealership, then you need to document how you will nurture leads and close deals.

Operations

Locations & Facilities

INSTRUCTIONS: Describe your company's physical locations. This might be your office, store locations, manufacturing plants, storage facilities — whatever is relevant to your business. How much space do you have available, and how well will it meet your current and future needs?

Technology

INSTRUCTIONS: Describe any important software, hardware, or other information technology that you use now or plan to use later to operate your business. That might include a point-of-sale system to take payments, an e-commerce engine for your website, a CRM solution for managing your pipeline, marketing tools for generating leads, and so on.

Equipment & Tools

INSTRUCTIONS: List any specialty equipment that you have or plan to acquire to do your

work. This is an important component of the business plan for many industrial companies.

Milestones & Metrics

Milestones

INSTRUCTIONS: List your key milestones and the dates that you hope to accomplish them by. If you've already accomplished key goals for your business, list them here as evidence that your business is getting traction – in other words, it's getting positive attention from potential customers.

Key Metrics

INSTRUCTIONS: Explain which performance metrics are most important for understanding

how your business is doing. What does success mean for you, and how will you know it when

you see it?

Company

Overview

INSTRUCTIONS: Use this area to specify who owns your company. If there are multiple

owners, describe each of them and how much of an ownership stake they have. Also, identify

your company's legal structure. Is it a sole proprietorship — that is, just you working for

yourself? Or a partnership, such as a limited-liability corporation (LLC) or partnership (LLP),

where the profits pass through to the partners involved? Or a nonprofit organization? Or a proper

S- or C-type corporation with its own tax obligations and the rest?

Team

Management Team

INSTRUCTIONS: List the members of the management team, including yourself. Describe each person's skills and experience and what they will be doing for the company. It's OK if you don't have everyone for a complete management team yet. In that case, make sure to identify gaps in your team that you intend to fill over time.

Advisors

INSTRUCTIONS: Describe any mentors, investors, former professors, industry or subject-matter experts, knowledgeable friends or family members, small-business counselors, or others who can help you as a business owner.

Financial Plan

Forecast

Key Assumptions

INSTRUCTIONS: Describe how you came up with the values in your financial forecast. Did you project your revenue based on past results, market research, your best guess at how many people who visit your store and what percentage of them might buy, or some other method? What kind of growth are you assuming? What are your key hires and notable expenses? What level of profit do you expect to generate?

Revenue by Month

INSTRUCTIONS: Include a chart that shows your projected revenue.

Expenses by Month

INSTRUCTIONS: Include a chart that shows your projected expenses.

Net Profit (or Loss) by Year

INSTRUCTIONS: Include a chart that shows your projected expenses.

Financing

Use of Funds

INSTRUCTIONS: If your forecast includes loans, investments, or other financing, use this space

to explain what you plan to do with that money.

Sources of Funds

INSTRUCTIONS: Describe your financing plans. Are you investing your own money in the

business? Do you have a credit card or line of credit? What other types of funds — personal or

business loans, equity investments from others, etc. — do you expect to receive and when? If

you do not have the full detail of future financing worked out yet, that is understandable. Just

explain what you do know and when you expect to sort out the details.

Statements

Profit and loss

Trading Profit and Loss Account Format

Net sales		100,000
Net purchases	46,000	
Beginning inventory	8,000	
Ending inventory	- 9,000	
Cost of goods sold		**45,000**
Gross profit		**55,000**
Expenses		48,000
Other income		5,000
Net profit		**12,000**

Trading

Profit and loss

INSTRUCTIONS: Provide a summary of your financial forecast here.

Balance sheet

NAME OF THE ORGANIZATION
BALANCE SHEET
-----Date-----

Liabilities		$	Assets		$
Capital fund	XXXX		Building	XXXX	
Add: Surplus	XXXX	XXXX	Less: Depreciation	XXXX	XXXX
Subscription received in advance		XXXX	Furniture	XXXX	
Outstanding wages		XXXX	Less: Depreciation	XXXX	XXXX
Outstanding salaries		XXXX			
			Sports equipment	XXXX	
			Less: Depreciation	XXXX	XXXX
			Subscription receivable		XXXX
			Prepaid rent		XXXX
			Cash		XXXX
Total liabilities		XXXX	Total assets		XXXX

INSTRUCTIONS: Include your balance sheet here.

Cash flow statement

Format of a Cash Flow Statement

Cash Flow Statement for the year ended		
Cash Flows from Operating Activities:		
Receipts from customers	xx	
Payments to suppliers and employees	(xx)	
Dividends received	xx	
Interest received	xx	
Payment of interest and borrowing costs	(xx)	
Income Tax paid	(xx)	
Net Cash from (used in) Operating Activities:		xx
Cash Flows from Investing Activities:		
Proceeds from sale of property, plant & equipment	xx	
Payment for property, plant & equipment	(xx)	
Net Cash from (used in) Investing Activities:		xx

INSTRUCTIONS: Include your cash flow statement here.

STRATEGY

PRODUCTS

SOLUTION

TARGET

WORK

TEAMWORK

GOAL

BUSINESS PLAN

MARKETING

SUCCESS

IDEAS LEADERSHIP

SERVICE

COMMUNICATION

INNOVATION

FINANCE

INSPIRE

PROFIT

ORGANISATION

PEOPLE

CONCLUSION.

By now you should know how to:

- Write a one page business plan

- Write a business plan

- Complete financial statements

- Market your business

- Start a successful business

Procrastination is the thief of time, if you have a business idea start brainstorming and writing your business plan. This book has equipped you with all the information, strategies and necessary skills that you need in order to commence an organized and productive business. Business makes the world go round these days, everything around you can be turned into a business, it takes planning, effort, determination and focus to turn the bricks around you into a house. People are always looking for shortcuts to succeed in business but in the words of a businesswoman, Nicki Minaj, "you've got to have real skill and work for that". There is no shortcut in starting a successful business, you have to invest yourself in it, plan and be strategic. Start building your business now, you have everything it takes to succeed!

ABOUT THE AUTHOR

Brendon Thutso is a businessman, IT specialist and an author. One of his most notable businesses is his multi department enterprise Brendata store, which he founded in West New York in New Jersey in 2019. He has written 3 books.. His debut book being a poetry book titled, "to my crush". That book reached the top spot of the best selling romance books on amazon and received a nomination for best graphic romance in the kindle awards of 2019. Many quotes were derived from that book. His second book is titled "wonders will never end". This is a story book which peaked at number 15 on the best selling books on amazon. His new book, "Business acumen : Business plan" is an educational and informative book on how to be successful in business. It encompasses how to write a business plan, how to appeal to funders for a loan and how to be strategic and skillful in business.